Do You See Me, God?
Prayers for Young Children

Chariot Books™
David C. Cook Publishing Co.

Elspeth Campbell Murphy
Illustrated by Bill Duca

Chariot Books is an imprint of David C. Cook Publishing Co.
David C. Cook Publishing Co., Elgin, Illinois 60120
David C. Cook Publishing Co., Weston, Ontario

DO YOU SEE ME, GOD?

Book design by Dawn Lauck

First Printing, 1989

Printed in Singapore
94 93 92 91 90   5 4 3 2

Library of Congress Cataloging-in-Publication Data
Murphy, Elspeth Campbell.
    Do you see me, God? / by Elspeth Campbell Murphy; illustrated by Bill
Duca.
        p.   cm.
    Summary: A collection of prayer-poems to God, with related Bible verses,
under such titles as "Watch me, God! Watch me!" and "Bad Mood."
        ISBN 1-55513-457-2
    1. Children—Prayer-books and devotions—English. [1. Prayer books and
devotions.] I. Duca, Bill, ill. II. Title.
BV4870.M84 1989
242′.82—dc19   88-27445
                                                                         CIP
                                                                          AC

Dear Grown-Up,

Something happens for us when we look at God through a young child's imaginative eyes: Our own faith is freshened. That's why the Scripture verses are included—for your own meditation. For example, in one prayer-poem the child tells God about an "owie." And the accompanying Scripture (Psalm 103:13, 14) reminds us, as adults, that God is our sympathetic Father, who wants to hear all about our "owies," too.

So share this book with your young child. And may God richly bless you both!

ECM

WATCH ME, GOD! WATCH ME!

Watch me, God! Watch me!
I can jump off
The next-to-the-top step
Of my grandmother's porch.
And—if I stand on tiptoe—
I can touch the lowest branch of that tree.
And listen, God, listen!
I can say the whole alphabet
(Except sometimes I get mixed up around LMNOP).
And—and—
I love it that You're always here, God!
Watch me!

O Lord, you have searched me
and you know me.
You know when I sit and when
I rise;
you perceive my thoughts
from afar....
You hem me in—behind and
before;
you have laid your hand
upon me.

PSALM 139:1, 2, 5

HIDING

I hung a blanket
From chair to chair,
And suddenly—
I wasn't there!
Everyone's wondering
Where I went.
Do You see me, God?
I'm in my tent!

He who dwells in the shelter of
the Most High
will rest in the
shadow of the Almighty.
I will say of the Lord, "He is my
refuge and my fortress,
my God, in whom I trust."

PSALM 91:1, 2

GOING BANANAS

Bananas, bananas!
God made bananas!
God made bananas,
And I LOVE bananas!

Just fill my bandanna
With a bunch of bananas—
I'll eat them for lunch
On my way to Montana!

Praise the Lord, O my soul,
and forget not all his benefits—
who satisfies your desires with
good things
so that your youth is
renewed like the eagle's.
PSALM 103:2, 5

WATER! WATER!

Do You know what I *love*, God?
Drinking fountains!

Of course, sometimes the water tastes mineraly,
And sometimes it's warm and yukky.
And sometimes the fountain's too high to reach.
But sometimes—if I'm lucky—
There are steps up the side
And a lever to hold
And out splashes water, clear and cold!
And You'd think I was almost dying of thirst—
I slurp, until I almost burst.
Then I come up for air
With a happy grin,
With water running down my chin.

Do You know what I *love*, God?
Drinking fountains!
I'd climb a mountain
For a drinking fountain!

I spread out my hands to you;
my soul thirsts for you like a
parched land.

PSALM 143:6

BRAND-NEW SHOES

Look, God!
Look at my
Look at my
Look at my
SHOES!

New shoes
New shoes
Skip-to-the-moon shoes!

Look at my
Look at my
Look at my
SHOES!

How beautiful on the mountains
    are the feet of those who
        bring good news,
who proclaim peace,
    who bring good tidings,
    who proclaim salvation,
who say to Zion,
    "Your God reigns!"
ISAIAH 52:7

NOT MY BIRTHDAY

I'm just a person who came to the party—
It's somebody else's birthday today.
Somebody else gets to blow out the candles.
But You know what, God?
That's OK!

Be devoted to one another in
brotherly love. Honor one
another above yourselves.

ROMANS 12:10

TODAY IS THE DAY

Today is the day!
Today is the day!
Hip, hip, hooray!
Today is the day!

It's finally here!
It's finally here!
Three cheers! Three cheers!
It's *finally* here!

Cake and candles!
Presents galore!
Streamers on trees!
Balloons on the door!

I know I'm going a little wild—
But You see, God,
I'm the Birthday Child!

You anoint my head with oil;
   my cup overflows.
                    PSALM 23:5b

GOD BLESS

God,
You know when I pray—
All those people I mention?
That's so You'll give them
Some special attention!

In the same way, the Spirit helps us in our weakness. We do not know what we ought to pray for, but the Spirit himself intercedes for us with groans that words cannot express. And he who searches our hearts knows the mind of the Spirit, because the Spirit intercedes for the saints in accordance with God's will.

ROMANS 8:26, 27

BAD MOOD

You know what, God?
I'm feeling a little sad today,
Grumpy, whiny, mad today.
When will a good mood
Come out to play?

Why are you downcast,
O my soul?
Why so disturbed within me?
Put your hope in God,
for I will yet praise him,
my Savior and my God.

PSALM 42:11

FROM THE TOP OF THE SLIDE

Look at me, God!

All by myself
I climbed up the slide.
I can see far and wide
From the top of the slide!

From the top of the slide
I can see far and wide!

Can You see
Wide and far?
From where You are?

The earth is the Lord's, and
everything in it,
the world, and all who
live in it.

PSALM 24:1

GOD'S DOGS

I think You must like making things, God.
Take, for example, dogs. You make:

Collies and Scotties and cocker spaniels!
Schnauzers, Chihuahuas, and chow chows!
Pekingese, beagles, and golden retrievers!
Great Danes, Dalmatians, and greyhounds!
Irish setters! Yorkshire terriers!
German shepherds! Saint Bernards!
Dachshunds, poodles, Doberman pinschers. . .
Well, I *could* go on and on.

I think You must like making things, God.
Take, for example, dogs.
You never make just one or two kinds;
When You make dogs, You make—*DOGS*!!!

How many are your works,
O Lord!
In wisdom you made them all;
the earth is full of
your creatures.

PSALM 104:24

OW!

I fell down, God—and got an owie!
The cat said, "Meowie!
Such a bad owie!"
The dog said, "Bow-*wow*ie!
Just look at that owie!"
"Daddy!" I cried. "I got an owie!"
He said, "And howie!"

As a father has compassion on
    his children,
    so the Lord has compassion
    on those who fear him;
for he knows how we are
    formed,
    he remembers that
    we are dust.

PSALM 103:13, 14

DECISIONS! DECISIONS!

What do *You* think, God?

This morning for breakfast
We went out to eat,
And they asked if I wanted
A booster seat.

I'm not a big kid. . .
I'm not a baby. . .
Decisions! Decisions!
I told them—"Maybe."

And Jesus grew in wisdom and
stature, and in favor with God
and men.

LUKE 2:52

LITTLE RED CAR

Oh, I'm off for a ride
In my little red car
In my little red car
But I won't go far—
Just the nearest star!

Will You watch for me, God—
As I drive by
As I drive by
In a car that can fly
Through the twinkling sky?

Oh, if I had a car
That really flew
That really flew
You know what I'd do?
Come visit You!

Dear friends, now we are
children of God, and what we
will be has not yet been made
known. But we know that when
he appears, we shall be like him,
for we shall see him as he is.

I JOHN 3:2